CONGRA⬛⬛⬛S
YOU ARE GOING TO HAVE A
BABY

Breaking the Bondage of Barrenness
200 Prayer Points

MATTHEW ASHIMOLOWO

MATTYSON MEDIA

© 1998 Matthew Ashimolowo

Mattyson Media Company
P. O. Box 12961
London
E15 1UR

Bible quotes are from the King James Bible unless otherwise stated.

ISBN 1-874646-21-X

CONTENTS

Chapter 1

BARRENNESS

The Hebrew word *"agar"* from which barrenness is derived has several meanings. It could mean to hold back as if causing a delay or to shut up something so that whatever is in it does not come out or could also mean to lock up as if to store away until an appropriate time.

"Agar" also means

- to hold back so as to cause a delay.
- to store up until an appropriate time of release.
- sterility at the vegetative organs.

It is to dam or seal up to prevent a flow. In another sense, it could mean to have no fruit. The word *"agar"* could also mean to pluck up by the root so as to cause to die or abort. It covers the area of miscarriage.

Another meaning of the word could carry the connotation of being sterile at the regenerative organ. Maybe a more definitive way of saying that is impotence. *"Agar"* could apply to both male or female. In other words, there is no specification as to who is barren. It could be a man or a woman as modern science has since confirmed.

Finally, *"agar"* could also mean to hamstring in order to choke life out of a thing or somebody.

These definitions of barrenness show that it is not the plan or the will of God for people not to receive their blessing. The scripture clarifies this in the book of Exodus 23:26;

> *"no one shall suffer miscarriage or be barren in your land. I will fulfil the number of your days."*

In this book, we will establish the fact that barrenness, while often recognised as a problem of childbirth could also be applicable to two other areas. There can be barrenness in the church resulting in the church failing to achieve its original purpose or the destined reason for its establishment. Barrenness could extend to the area of people's finances so that they do not experience the kind of abundance which God intends for them.

We shall be looking at the causes of the various strands of barrenness and the possible cure for them in more detail.

Congratulation, you are going to have a baby!

Chapter 2

THE DEBILITATING CONDITION OF BARRENNESS

1.) Certainly from scripture, barrenness leaves those who experience it hurt, in pain and probably leaves a scar on their heart for the rest of their life.

The first of the debilitating conditions of barrenness is the fact that the barren womb is never satisfied. *"Therefore because a womb that is barren is never satisfied, it leaves the heart broken".*

2.) **Such people are unhappy and lack joy.** This is very apparent from the way they carry themselves.

3.) **Barrenness in the land of Israel and in certain cultures was regarded as a terrible plight.** Many times, women were driven to the edge of suicide. Instead of receiving sympathy and care, they were made to go through embarrassing experiences all in the name of desiring a child. In some extreme cases, a woman might even be required to carry a kid goat on her back into a market place for people to see her. That way it is believed that she will end up having a child.

4.) **In bible times every Jewish woman knew of the biblical promise of the virgin birth.**

> *"And I will put enmity between thee and the woman, and between thy seed and her seed; it shall bruise thy head, and thou shall bruise his heel." Genesis 3:15*

Most women thought that the promised child would come through them. There was an expectation of a miraculous pregnancy and whenever there was a delay, such women thought that the prophecy was about to be fulfilled through them.

5.) **A barren woman needs constant assurance from her husband.** The level of insecurity expressed is very high for the fear that their husband may look for an alternative child elsewhere especially in the cultures where adoption is foreign.

6.) In the case of the Church, **a barren ministry or minister will produce barren lives.** There is no fruitfulness in such churches. New souls are not saved and there is no fresh testimony. There is no deliverance and they have a survival mentality.

7.) **Barrenness is often the root of a feeling that ones dreams have been shattered and may not come to pass.**

8.) **Barrenness brings a feeling of hopelessness** and the thought that things cannot change.

We should remember what the scriptures says *"with God all things are possible"* also, Hebrews 13:8 says - *"Jesus Christ is the same yesterday, today and forever"*.

9.) **There is fear of the cycles of life overtaking the barren.** In other words, the fear of the inability to give birth to a healthy child at a certain age, experiencing menopause and lack of eggs with which to reproduce.

10.) **A barren person is afraid that there might be** no one to leave an inheritance for.

11.) **Barrenness increases the anxiety of a person** making them more provocative in some environment, as we see in the next chapter.

Chapter 3

PHYSICAL BARRENNESS

SARAH - "JUSTIFIED BY FAITH"

Sarah stands out as the first recorded case of barrenness in the Bible. The wife of Abraham a man to whom God had promised that the nations of the world shall be blessed through him. His name suggests that he will be a father and by Sarah's name a mother. However, this was not their experience rather, it was the opposite.

It is interesting to note that despite the age of Sarah and her husband they exercised faith that God who had promised is able to make His grace abound to them. From Sarah's life we learn that God responds to faith in the midst of failure. Furthermore God is not bound by what usually happens.

Breakthrough is really when God makes the unusual to take place in our lives. God can stretch the limit and allow the impossible to happen. Sarah was ninety and with no hope of childbirth but God created the womb. If He says it's possible it cannot be reversed. As soon as she expressed faith Sarah worked her way into the list of the hall of faith in Hebrews chapter eleven.

She was the first woman listed because out of her barrenness came forth a great people. This was of course because of her step of faith. God wants us regardless of where we are, or what we have gone through to know that if He promised, it will come to pass you will still have that baby. Out of barrenness will come forth a testimony, out of Sarah's barrenness came forth a people and even today God can do it again.

It is safe to say Sarah's delay was by design. Out of it has come forth a message of resurrection in the face of death and the fact that if God can do it for Sarah there is nothing that we need that He would not provide. God and His word are the same. If He promises He will make it good. The complications which her delay brings was the fact that having waited for so long, Sarah acted in foolishness by trying to answer her own prayer providing an alternative source through which the child of promise was to come.

In this regard Sarah probably mirrored the truth that there is nothing as hard as waiting. You can make the mistake of helping God during your waiting more especially if there has been a delay. Sarah's action by providing Hagar as an alternative wife was common practice in Bible land in those days. God does not want us to walk by what is common practice but by faith.

As a result regret followed just as it follows today, when we push God aside and follow our own time table feeling that God has not responded as quick as He should. Passing Hagar to Abraham mirrors another truth, she probably felt that while God may answer prayer it could never happen to her. This probably informs her laughter when at ninety she had a visitation by three heavenly beings and one of them promising her a child.

In conclusion we learn from Sarah that we must

not try to make God's word come to pass in ways that are not in line with His direction. We also learn that faith is perfected by waiting and not by trying to figure things out ourselves. From Sarah we see that faith does not fail if God has to cause a resurrection He will do it.

HANNAH - "GOD'S GRACE IS SUFFICIENT"

All through the scriptures, we have account of women who were barren. Our study in this book will show how each woman represents different phases of experience a barren person may have to face or goes through. <u>Our second case study is Hannah</u>. Her name means "grace" and she is truly symbolic of grace as she faced extreme provocation and ridicule.

> *"And her adversary also provoked her sore, for to make her fret, because the LORD had shut up her womb."* I Samuel 1:6

Hannah was perpetually provoked and ridiculed and the scripture says her life was made miserable by the other woman. Hannah's problem was that she had no children, no fruit, no proof of marriage, by the mediterranean standards and no sign of such children coming at all. Hannah was married to a man who loved her. Her source of provocation was not from him.

Hannah's husband loved her but unfortunately, he thought that his love and wealth were supposed to replace the vacuum she felt for having no children.

> *"Then said Elkanah her husband to her, Hannah, why weepest thou? And why eatest thou not? And why is thy heart grieved? Am I not better to thee than ten sons?" I Samuel 1:8*

Hannah was also religious but there was no fruit to show for it.

Hannah cried with *"grace"* in the midst of provocation and it is possible that her *"grace"* was what led to her receiving, according to the scripture, *"a worthy portion of her husbands blessing"*.

Her husband's action suggested that he had faith in spite of the provocation and apparent absence of a child. He was not carried away by the tradition of his times which treated a barren woman as scum because she had no child.

Receiving a worthy portion, on the other hand could be so tempting to the point where you are satisfied with basic blessings. It is necessary for you to keep your eye on your greatest motivation which is the ultimate blessing. Whatever you do, do not get stuck on the basic blessing. Many barren people are in a situation like Hannah with a person whose provocation gets on their nerves by constantly reminding them of what they are trusting God for or by parading their own apparent blessings.

What should be the response of one who is trusting God for the fruit of the womb?

The best possible thing at such times is:

1.) **Attend church regularly.** David said *"one thing have I desired of the Lord, that will I seek after, to behold the beauty of the Lord, to enquire in His temple".* *Psalm 27:4*

2.) **Cry to God**. The bible says in Jeremiah 33:3 *"call upon me in the time of sorrow".*

3.) **Refuse to sit back and wallow in regret.** This will destroy your joy.

4.) **Do not confirm the prophecy of your enemies.** They think your life will fall apart; do not give them the joy of seeing it come to pass.

5.) **Do something unusual.**

Unusual actions provoke unusual results. Sow a seed to reap your harvest.

6.) **Pray increasingly.**

"And it came to pass, as she continued praying before the LORD, *that Eli marked her mouth." I Samuel 1:12*

7.) Worship reverently.

"And Hannah prayed, and said, My heart rejoiceth in the LORD, *mine horn is exalted in the* LORD: *my mouth is enlarged over mine enemies; because I rejoice in thy salvation.*

There is none holy as the LORD: *for there is none beside thee: Neither is there any rock like our God.*

Talk no more so exceedingly proudly; let not arrogancy come out of your mouth: for the LORD *is a God of knowledge, and by him actions are weighed.*

The bows of the mighty men are broken, and they that stumbled are girded with strength.

They that were full have hired out themselves for bread; and they that were hungry ceased: so that the barren hath born seven; and she that hath many children is waxed feeble.

The LORD *killeth, and maketh alive: he bringeth down to the grave, and bringeth up.*

The LORD *maketh poor, and maketh rich: he bringeth*

low, and lifteth up.

He raiseth up the poor out of the dust, and lifteth up the beggar from the dunghill, to set them among princes, and make them inherit the throne of glory: for the pillars of the earth are the LORD's, and he hath set the world upon them.

He will keep the feet of his saints, and the wicked shall be silent in darkness; for by strength shall no man prevail.

The adversaries of the LORD shall be broken to pieces; out of heaven shall he thunder upon them: the LORD shall judge the ends of the earth; and he shall give strength unto his king, and exalt the horn of his anointed." I Samuel 2:1-10

8.) **Sing aloud.**

9.) **Serve wholeheartedly.**
"And when she had weaned him, she took him up with her, with three bullocks, and one ephah of flour, and a bottle of wine, brought him unto the house of the LORD in shiloh: and the child was young.

And they slew a bullock, and brought the child to Eli." I Samuel 1:24-25

10.) **Think positively.**

11.) **Give faithfully.**

"And she said, O my Lord, as thy soul liveth, my Lord, I am the woman that stood by thee here, praying unto the LORD.

For this child I prayed; and the LORD hath given me my petition which I asked of him.

Therefore also I have lent him to the LORD; as long as he liveth he shall be lent to the LORD. And he worshipped the Lord there." I Samuel 1:26-28

Remember that when your *"Samuel"* grows up, he will be a child of destiny.

Hannah must have been told that her reproductive organ was sterile because the Hebrew word used in describing her suggests this.

"They that were full have hired out themselves for bread; and they that were hungry ceased: so that the barren that hath many children is waxed feeble.

The LORD killeth , and maketh alive: he bringeth down to the grave, and bringeth up" I Samuel 2:5-6

Her prayer reveals that her case was a divine intervention. Other than that, it was the kind of impotence that could not be cured by man.

> *"He will keep the feet of his saints, and the wicked*
> *shall be silent in darkness; for by strength shall no*
> *man prevail" I Samuel 2:9*

A barren person must look forward to that day when they will give a public testimony because such testimony encourages other people. Many people have drawn strength from the story of Hannah and have since trusted God knowing that because He had done it for others, he would do it for them.

> *"And she said, O my Lord, as thy soul liveth, my*
> *Lord, I am the woman that stood by thee here, praying*
> *unto the LORD.*
>
> *For this child I prayed; and the LORD hath given me*
> *my petition which I asked of him." I Samuel 1:26 - 27*

A barren person must be willing to let go of something to provoke God's blessing on them.

> *"Therefore also I have lent him to the LORD; as long*
> *as he liveth he shall be lent to the LORD. And he*
> *worshipped the Lord there." I Samuel 1:28*

If you are not willing to release what is in your hand, you will not receive what God has for you. To experience unusual blessing, you must take unusual steps. A sacrificial offering will always precede a supernatural favour.

A barren person must not only desire a baby but pray for a miracle child. After all, you have waited this long. God may cause delay because the child coming is a baby of destiny, once this happens other children will be born as well.

> "And the LORD Visited Hannah, so that she conceived, and bare three sons and two daughters. And the child Samuel grew before the LORD" I Samuel 2: 21

REBECCA - "INTERCESSION MAKES THE DIFFERENCE"

Rebecca's marriage could be described as made in heaven. She was married into a family which had a standing covenant with God and was highly loved by her husband -

However Rebecca was barren despite the prophetic blessing from her family.

> *"And they blessed Rebekah, and said unto her, Thou art our sister, be thou the mother of thousands of millions, and let thy seed possess the gate of those which hate them." Genesis 24:60*

Her family had prophesied into her life that her spiritual and natural children would posses the gates of their enemies.

The fulfilment seemed to evade her. Rebecca's demand on her husband and his subsequent action reveals another approach to breaking the cycle of barrenness which is <u>petitioning for a change</u>.

> <u>*"And Isaac entreated the LORD for his wife, because*</u>
> *she was barren: and the LORD was entreated of him,*

and Rebekah his wife conceived." Genesis 25:21

<u>The prayer of supplication</u> is a necessary step to remove impasse.

There are several kinds of prayer in the bible, the prayer of intercession or supplication can be repeated more than once. It is petitioning someone in authority orally or in written form, presenting your case for adjudication until there is a response. We can also rely on the Holy Spirit - to assist us.

> *"Likewise the Spirit also helpeth our infirmities: for we know not we should pray for as we ought: but the Spirit itself maketh intercession for us with groanings which cannot be uttered." Romans 8:26*

Help is also available from the Lord Jesus Christ *"we have an advocate with the Father, Jesus Christ the righteous"*.

SHUNAMMITE WOMAN - "IT IS NEVER TOO LATE"

"And it fell on a day, that Elisha passed to Shunem, where was a great woman; and she constrained him to eat bread. And so it was, that as oft as he passed by, he turned in thither to eat bread.

And she said unto her husband, Behold now, I perceive that this is an holy man of God, which passeth by us continually.

Let us make a little chamber, I pray thee, on the wall; and let us set for him there a bed, and a table, and a stool, and a candlestick: and it shall be, when he cometh to us, that he shall turn in thither.

And it fell on a day, that he came thither, and he turned into the chamber, and lay there.

And he said to Gehazi his servant, Call this Shunammite. And when he had called her, she stood before him.

And he said unto him, Say now unto her, Behold, thou hast been careful for us with all this care; what is to be done for thee? Wouldest thou be spoken for to the king, or to the captain of the host? And she answered, I dwell among mine own people.

> *And he said, What then is to be done for her? And Gehazi answered, Verily she hath no child, and her husband is old.*
>
> *And he said, Call her. And when he had called her, she stood in the door.*
>
> *And he said, About this season, according to the time of life, thou shalt embrace a son. And she said, Nay, my lord, thou man of God, do not lie unto thine handmaid" II King 4:8-16*

The story of the Shunammite woman in II Kings chapter 4 verse 8 confirms the truth that with "*God it is never too late*". Scriptures gives a background about her, a notable woman, wealthy, a comfortable life style, respected among her people with a big house and room to accommodate guests.

Having noticed a need in the life of Elisha; which is a place to have a break, unhampered and unhindered in his ministry, she provided the facilities. Elisha in turn wanting to reciprocate, asked his servant what could be done for her.

> *"And he said unto him, Say now unto her, <u>Behold,</u> thou hast been careful for us with all this care; what is to be done for thee? Wouldest thou be spoken for to the king, or to the captain of the host? And she*

> *answered, I dwell among mine people."*
> II Kings 4:13

The woman felt she had no need because she had all she wanted but there was a greater need - that of a child.

The response of this woman when Elisha told her she would embrace a child was that of *"I have no need"*.

A possible reason was because the problem has been there for long and she has decided to live with it. Furthermore, her husband was old therefore she felt not only would he have experienced a degree of impotence but was probably sterile as well. People like this are just fed up and try to cope without a child and in some cultures they adopt a child. Even in the process of the adoption, sometimes they may hurt the more because they may have fallen into the hands of bogus adoption agencies. The Shunammite woman had probably gone through this several times.

> *"And he said, About this season, according to the time of life, thou shalt embrace a son. And she said, Nay, my lord, thou man of God, do not lie unto thine hand maid."* II Kings 4:16

She had accepted her circumstance. The word circumstance is a Latin word but actually derived from two words which means *"circles of standing"*. People are limited because they are in circles of their own making.

She was not ready to express faith any more having done that several times and possibly in several meetings where she was prayed for. At this point in time the only thing the man of God succeeded in doing was to bring up an old desire.

Elisha stood his grounds; he said

> *"About this time next year, you shall embrace a son".*
> *II Kings 4:16*

Her response expresses her heartache *"No my lord, man of God, do not lie to your maidservant".* She must have been a victim of false hope and false prophecy.

Even in today's world the danger a person who is battling with barrenness or the absence of physical fruitfulness is that they believe all adverts, go to all deliverance meetings even if the doctrine and teaching of such people is wrong. If any one faces the challenge of unfruitfulness as in the case of the Shunammite woman, the possible step to take is;

1.) Do not be intimidated by the impossible. God says

> *"Behold I am the God of all flesh is there anything to hard for me?" Jeremiah 32:27*

> *"For I am the LORD, I change not; therefore ye sons of Jacob are not consumed." Malachi 3:6*

 2.) God may be planning something beyond your faith. God has a plan for your life and it is a good one.

> *"For I know the thoughts that I think toward you, saith the Lord, thoughts of peace, and not of evil, to give you an expected end." Jeremiah 29:11*

3.) Remember when faith stops working, God will use the element called time as in the case of Elizabeth. Faith obviously must be expressed but there is a point where hope deferred makes the heart grow weary. When faith gets low, the time for miracles gets closer. The Scripture makes us to understand that there is an <u>appointed time.</u>

> *"For the vision is yet for an appointed time, but at the end it shall speak, and not lie: though it tarry, wait for it ; because it will surely come." Habakkuk 2:3*

People have a habit of reminding God how old they are. As in the case of this woman. I am sure when you remind God of how old you are, He will remind you of how eternal He is.

4.) **Learn how to face tomorrow without the fear of yesterday**. Yesterday is gone and it will not come back. Do not let your past ruin your future, learn to face tomorrow without the fear of yesterday.

5.) **Remember that God did not bless Abraham via his reproductive organs but by resurrection power.**

> *"(As it is written, I have made thee a father of many nations,) before him whom he believed, even God, who quickeneth the dead, and calleth those things which be not as though they were.*
>
> *Who against hope believed in hope, that he might become the father of many nations, according to that which was spoken, So shall thy seed be.*
>
> *And being not weak in faith, he considered not his own body now dead, when he was about an hundred years old, neither yet the deadness of Sarah's womb:"*
> *Romans 4:17 - 19*

6.) **Understand that when a miracle is due, nothing is as powerful as it.** God is still true to His word, He said, *"You shall bear fruit in old age"*. So, let us remember the *"set time"* when we are challenged with thing that seem to have been evading one for so long.

When it seems to be to late, remember there is a time for you to be healed, delivered, resurrected from a dead situation. There is a time for your open door, a time for your net to be let down to draw in the multitude of fish. When you feel it is late, remember, it is the right time that matters.

ELIZABETH - "WAIT FOR YOUR APPOINTED TIME"

Another example of fruit bearing in old age is the case of Elizabeth the mother of John the Baptist; the wife of a priest who lived in the hillsides of Judæa and served in the temple in Jerusalem. Her experience is also reflective of the attitude people put on when delay appears to become a denial. People are quick to forget that the scriptures can never be broken, delays are never denials.

When the angel of the God appeared to Zãcharias and said,

"Do not be afraid Zãcharias for your prayer is answered"

His response was *"How can I know this, I am an old man, my wife is advanced in age"*.

As if he did not expect the prayer to be answered or had given up and accepted the pain of an absence of a child.

Particularly, the blessing which was promised them by way of John the Baptist was unique in the sense that Elizabeth's pregnancy was rightly timed. It could not have been earlier, neither could it have been later because the child whom she bore was to be the fore runner of the Lord. If he had been born at the time they desired, he would have been too old for the ministry he was called for and if he had come later, he would have been too young.

This registers the truth that some people who experience delay, need to understand also that some circumstances are for specific reasons and they will experience joy on the appointed day. God is meticulous about vision and that includes yours. Well, you must know that your vision and its fulfilment is for an appointed time.

> *"For the vision is yet for an appointed time; but at the end it shall speak, and not lie: though it tarry, wait for it; because it will surely come, it will not tarry." Habakkuk 2:3*

This kind of case show how glory is *"born"* in the womb of barrenness. Who would have known that Elizabeth, and Zācharias, old people, would one day be the parents of a child of glory.

So it is not what people do right but it is the time that is right and since this case was for the glory of

God, the breakthrough had to be called by its proper name. John, the name given by an angel of God means *"the gift of God"*. It was not the making of man, it was the working of God. If your breakthrough is from God, let the glory stay with Him. Do not praise [1]*IVF* or any other method which you may be trying. You may experience a blessing through medical help but still give the glory to whom it is due; the only one who would give you a child, the Lord Jesus Christ.

[1]*IVF* - Invitro Fertilization

Chapter 4

MEDICAL CAUSES

OF BARRENNESS

OR INFERTILITY

Information is necessary for the possession of a blessing. You can only be set free by the truth you know. In this part of this book, I listed and defined some of the causes of infertility from a medical point of view.

FEMALE FACTORS

1. Ovulatory Disorders

Premature ovarian failure - ovary fails to mature into adulthood.

Polycystic ovary syndrome - This is a situation in which the ovary develops a lot of cysts which affects the regular production of hormones.

Congenital abnormalities - Deformities from birth which affects production of hormones.

Hormonal problems that affect the ovaries from other endocrine organs in the body are hyperprolactinaemia (high prolactin in blood), low hormonal influence from the hypothalamus and pituitary glands which help to regulate the ovarian function (mainly FSH and LH)

Weight loss as in Anorexia Nervosa, for ovulatory cycles to be maintained, fat should account for at least 22% of total body weight. Fat seems to be an important factor and necessary for regular ovulation and menstruation.

Exercise - related ovarian disorder can occur for the same reason as for weight loss.

Obesity on the other hand is associated with less frequent ovulation and menstruation.

2. Tubal Blockage or Damage

The fallopian tube receives the egg from the ovary, if it is damaged or blocked it affects the transfer of the egg into the uterus. It is also the place where the egg and the sperm meet. Tubal damage is caused mainly by previous infections. For example gonorrhoea and chlamydia infections, including Tuberculosis.

3. Endemetriosis

This is the occurrence of endometrial tissue, which is the lining of the uterus in other parts of the body like the bladder or intestines. It is said to cause infertility or caused by infertility.

4. Cervical Mucus Problems

This might prevent the penetration of the sperm into the uterus (womb), either by being too thick or by producing antibodies that destroy the sperm.

5. Rare Uterine Abnormalities

Wombs that are abnormally shaped or positioned could cause infertility.

MALE FACTORS

This represents about 19% of the causes of infertility. Male infertility boils down to the production of sperm. There could be a complete absence, which is called a Zoospermia, a low production called Oligospermia. Other problems could be with the mobility of the sperm called asthenozoospermia.

It could be a problem with the morphology, which is called teratozoospermia. This is related to the way the sperm is shaped.

Causes are:

1. **Coital difficulties**, that is, erectile impotence of psychogenic, vascular or neurological origin.

2. **Past sexually transmitted diseases** that have affected the testis or the pathway of the sperm flow.

3. **History of mumps orchitis** - orchitis is the

inflammation of the testis.

4. **History of undescended testis** - There is a particular temperature in which spermatogenesis should take place. If the testis is undescended for a long time in the early years or adulthood, it stays within the abdomen, which has a higher temperature than the scrotum.

5. **History of scrotal, inguinal, prostate or bladder surgery**.

6. **Any form of testicular injury or trauma** - Radiation, chemotherapy drugs for cancer, toxic chemicals can all damage the testis thus affecting the production of sperm.

7. **Filarial worms** - These block the lymph vessels and cause elephantiasis of the scrotum.

8. *Alcoholics and drug addicts* also experience a general suppression in fertility both for male and female.

Chapter 5

SPIRITUAL BARRENNESS

SIGNS OF A BARREN CHURCH

Barrenness could be a physical challenge but, it is of a greater consequence when it shows up in a church. How do you recognise a barren church? The following things become obvious in a church that has become spiritually barren:

1.) **No souls are saved at the altar**.

They have no fresh souls coming to know the Lord.

2.) Holding on to old testimony.

Members of such a local church talk of the good old days and make statements like *"I remember when this church used to be packed"* or *"I remember when this church used to be one big family"*.

3.) They develop a maintenance mentality and not a pioneer mentality.

The barren church only endeavours to keep things running and does not try to break new grounds.

4.) No miracles.

There is no fresh testimony and nothing happens that is of particular significance. Acts of the Apostles 3:9

5.) No sign of new life.

In every home where there is fruitfulness, it is either that the children have grown up and if they have not, there is a sign of the presence of children and new life. The same thing applies in a church. There ought to be things happening in the new converts class or the baptismal class which are the maternity wards of the vibrant church.

6.) **No new vision.**

Nothing new; the vision has become stale and they are now suffering from HIV - *"Having Insufficient Vision"*.

7.) **Finances dry up.**

No souls get saved therefore no one is being discipled and because there is no discipleship programme, finances are not coming in.

8.) **Mass emigration of the people.**

While Proverbs 29:18 says *"where there is not vision the people perish"*, in the case of the barren church, the people move parish.

9.) **There are signs of ageing, sickness and discomfort**.

Such sign in a local church may be both physical and spiritual. The building is ageing from lack of repair and the equipment are sagging and nothing seems to be working. Sickness and discomfort become prevalent in the church with no one making an effort to reach out and minister to the sick.

10.) **No expansion program.**

The church dwindles and there is no effort to expand in either infrastructure or spiritual program.

11.) **Problems which accompany growth are none existent.**

Growing churches also have their own problems; parking, crowd control, meeting and greeting, emptying the building and re-parking for another service. The ringing of telephone in the church by people who need help, counselling, prayer, et cetera. All these are absent in a barren church. As a matter of fact, a barren church is more of a ghost town from Monday to Saturday.

12.) **Leadership ceases to grow**.

The people have no vision to direct their energy, leadership ceases to grow and in effect begins to turn its energy at one another.

13.) **The quest for the knowledge of God wanes**.

In every growing church there is always the buzz. Older Christians have their faith kept alive because new believers express such hunger that makes older Christians not to be complacent. In a barren church, the opposite is the case.

14.) **The spirit of God no longer strives with them.**

God said to Noah that *"the spirit of God will no longer strive with those who have resisted Him"*. Nothing is as enjoyable and as tough as the Holy Spirit striving with you and reminding you of your need for change.

15.) **Only externals features suggests that it is a church.**

Where such a church exists and occupies a building with architecture features, that becomes the only symbolism of the church. Other than that there is no liveliness, members are not proud to tell their friends of their church.

16.) **Loss of first love.**

Since there is nothing to challenge the people, neither is a lot happening, they become lukewarm loose their first love. Sometimes we remember how our first love made us go all out witnessing, and inviting our friends to know the Lord.

17.) **Spiritually impotent.**

The Hebrew word for impotence *"agar"* could also mean sterile at the point of reproduction. Sterility is a problem of a barren church and because of its impotence; in message and service, that there cannot be reproduction.

18.) **No 'stirring' of ones self to take hold of the Lord.**

The cry of intercessors ceases in such a church. The enemy has come in and snuffed out the power and the life. As no one is making an effort to take hold of the Lord, the python spirit could have come in, causing more confusion. This is an imminent danger.

19.) **It sends out feelers.**

These feelers say *"Visitors are not welcomed"*. Barren churches have members whose actions, speeches and relational style suggests that visitors are not welcomed. The few people remaining seem to be holding the fort and the ground therefore, new talents who could have rejuvenated the church are not totally welcomed.

20.) **Preservation of sacred cows**.

In this case things which ought to have been jettisoned in order for the church to do well are kept as if they are necessary for the progress of the church. The church begins to dig its own grave and almost goes into oblivion, because it will not kill sacred cows, that is, vision and ideas that are not working.

THE CAUSE OF SPIRITUAL BARRENNESS

MICHAL

In the book of Second Samuel chapter 6 verses 16-23

"And it was so, that when they that bare the ark of the LORD had gone six paces, he sacrificed oxen and fatlings.

And David danced before the LORD with all his might; and David was girded with a linen ephod.

So David and all the house of Israel brought up the ark of the LORD with shouting, and with the sound of the trumpet.

And as the ark of the LORD came into the city of David, Michal Saul's daughter looked through a window, and saw king David leaping and dancing before the Lord; and she despised him in her heart.

And they brought in the ark of the LORD, and set it in his place, in the midst of the tabernacle that David had pitched for it: and David offered burnt offerings and peace offerings before the LORD.

And as soon as David had made an end of offering burnt offerings and peace offerings, he blessed the people in the name of the Lord of hosts.

And he dealt among all the people, even among the whole multitude of Israel, as well to the women as men, to every one a cake of bread, and a good piece of fish, and a flagon of wine. So all the people departed every one to his house.

Then David returned to bless his household. And Michal the daughter of Saul came out to meet David, and said, How glorious was the king of Israel today, who uncovered himself today in the eyes of the handmaids of his servants, as one of the vain fellows shamelessly uncovereth himself!

And David said unto Michal, It was before the LORD, *which chose me before thy father, and before all his house, to appoint me ruler over the people of the* LORD, *over Israel: therefore will I play before the* LORD.

And I will yet be more vile than thus, and will be base in mine own sight: and of the maidservants which thou hast spoken of, of them shall I be had in honour.

Therefore Michal the daughter of Saul had not child unto the day of her death"

We have the remarkable story of David's wife Michal, Saul's daughter. David wanted the glory of the Lord to be restored in Jerusalem while Saul did not care. Shortly after David regained the throne, he made an effort to bring back the Ark of the Lord to Jerusalem.

David had gone to pick the Ark of the Lord to bring it to Jerusalem with dancing and great celebration. From Michal's reaction it was very obvious that she despised what God approved.

God wanted glory, Michal wanted vainglory; God wanted praise, she belittled the work of God.

We read in II Samuel 6:23 of her barrenness. *"Therefore, Michal the daughter of Saul had not children till the end of her death. "*

She is symbolic of barren churches because the verse we have read links her barrenness to her spiteful behaviour. She mocked what God appreciated. Her problem as in the case of many churches is traceable to disbelieving, or despising what God is doing and what He values. Some cases of barrenness are not gynaecological but spiritual.

The same thing is applicable to local churches. The barrenness of the local church is avoidable.

Some causes are:

1.) Despising biblical way of worship.

It is necessary for the local church to celebrate the Lord and not ridicule the biblical way of worship like lifting up of holy hands in worship.

2.) Do not despise prophecy. As the scripture teaches.

3.) Do not despise godly praise.

The scripture says *"whoso offereth praise glorifieth me: and to him that ordereth his conversation aright will I shew the salvation of God"*. Psalm 50:32

4.) Do not despise godly preaching.

In other words, celebrate the message without preference for certain ministers.

5.) Do not despise godly chastisement.

The scripture says *"My son, despise not the chastening of the LORD; neither be weary of his correction: for whom the LORD loveth he correcteth; even as a father the son in whom he delighteth"* Proverbs 3:11-12.

6.) **Do not despise the days of small beginnings.**

These are things we are told in scripture not to despise and when such instruction is flaunted, barrenness becomes the consequence for the local church.

7.) **Do not despise servants of God.**

When a local church withholds and refuses to adequately remunerate its Pastor or if a visiting minister was not given the offerings raised in his name, it could stand against the local church.

Individuals may have spited a servant of God, if for some reason they have been rebellious and refuse correction and thus behaved or spoke against the servant of God.

THE CURE FOR SPIRITUAL BARRENNESS

In the book of Psalms 1:2 the scripture talks of meditation. It emphasises the necessity for meditation in the word of God day and night.

> *"Blessed is the man that walketh not in the counsel of the ungodly, nor standeth in the way of sinners, nor sitteth in the seat of the scornful.*
>
> *But his delight is in the law of the Lord; and in his law doth he meditate day and night.*
>
> *And he shall be like a tree planted by the rivers of water, that bringeth forth his fruit in his season; his leaf also shall not wither; and whatsoever he doeth shall prosper."* Psalm 1:1-3

1.) **Meditation is necessary for us to be able to fertilise the seed of our vision** so that it comes to fruition.

2.) **Meditation makes and moulds your personality.** As you dwell in the word of God, it begins to shape you world view.

3.) **Meditation is necessary because it reveals eventually what you are made of.** Jesus said out of the abundance of the heart the mouth speaketh so if you want to speak the counsel of God you have to meditate on it. Take it in and then mutter it to yourself.

4.) Meditation gives you Gods view of a situation.

In other words an adequate dose of God's word changes your perspective, it gives you a good view of a situation and not how the devil wishes it to be.

5.) Meditation helps you have a balanced view of a situation. A million voices of satan cannot erode or erase the powerful truth of God's word. We read about sowing seed in Genesis 26:12

"Then Isaac sowed in that land and reaped in the same year a hundredfold and God blessed him". As a result of sowing seed, harvest followed for Isaac and it was a maximum output.

6.) Meditation results in a maximum output. There may be other steps you need to take to experience spiritual fruitfulness in the church and in your personal life. Direction comes from the word of God so we emphasise the necessity to stay in the word as an antidote to barrenness.

Let your mouth meditate on the wisdom of God. Meditation is like *"chewing the curd"*. This symbolises staying in the word of God until it bears fruit.

7.) Meditation means repeating God's word to yourself. This is described in the first Psalm as *"a person who is planted by a river"* he is exposed to continuous moisture as such bears fruit all the time.

Staying in the word of God gives you spiritual moisture for fruitfulness.

David uses the illustration of a tree by the river which suggests that your season is not determined by what goes on around you. Being planted by the river it meant it could bear fruit in an out of season.

The result is described in Psalm 1:3 - *"You shall be like a tree planted by the rivers of water that brings forth its fruit in its season whose leaf shall also shall not wither and whatever he doeth shall prosper"*. This passage of scripture suggests:

1.) Success will attend what you do.

2.) You will do well in all your undertakings.

3.) Prosper in all things.

4.) You will accomplish all you set out to do.

5.) What you do will come to maturity.

Chapter 6

FINANCIAL BARRENNESS

THE CAUSES:

The book of Haggai gives a broad picture of the cause, consequence and cure for financial barrenness. It was written as a prophetic word in 520 BC to the Jews who had come back from Babylonian captivity. Upon arriving back they started building the temple of the Lord but at some point grew weary, left it uncompleted and focused on their own building. Consequently, things became difficult for them and they wondered why. This shows that financial hardship could arise from:

1.) **lack of time to serve the Lord.**

> *" Thus speaketh the* LORD *of hosts, saying, This people say, The time is not come, the time that the Lord's house should be built." Haggai 1:2*

2.) **unwillingness to build the kingdom of God.**

3.) **neglect for the things of the Lord.**

> *"Is it time for you, O ye, to dwell in your ceiled houses, and this house lie waste?" Haggai 1:4*

4.) **preference of your personal security to the well being of the ministry and the things of God.**

> *"Ye looked for much, and lo, it came to little; and when ye brought it home, I did blow upon it. Why? Saith the Lord of hosts. Because of mine house that is waste, and ye run every man unto his own house." Haggai 1:9*

5.) **wasted calling, gifting, blessing and purpose of God for one's life**.

> *"Ye looked for much, and lo, it came to little; and when ye brought it home, I did blow upon it. Why? Saith the Lord of hosts. Because of mine house that is waste, and ye run every man unto his own house." Haggai 1:9*

6.) **refusal to shown mercy and love.**

7.) **withheld tithe. God therefore brings a curse on whatever is left.**

> *"Ye are cursed with a curse: for ye have rubbed me, even this whole nation.*
>
> *Bring ye all the tithes into the storehouse, that there may be meat in mine house, and prove me now herewith, saith the lord of hosts, if I will not open you the windows of heaven, and pour you out a blessing, that there shall not be room enough to receive it."*
> *Malachi 3:9 - 10*

There are many other reasons why there could be financial bondage but the paramount is neglecting the work of God while focusing on you own personal benefit.

17 CONSEQUENCES OF FINANCIAL BARRENNESS

Where the work of the Lord has been abandoned or there is unfaithfulness in giving, tithing or ministering to members of the household of the faith:

1.) **There will be poor results.**

"Since those days were, when one came to an heap of twenty measures, there were but ten: when one came to the pressfat for to draw out fifty vessels out of the press, there were but twenty.

I smote you with blasting and with mildew and with hail in all the labours of your hands; yet ye turned not to me saith the LORD.*"   Haggai 2:16-17*

2.) **Unsatisfied quest.**

"Ye have sown much, and ring in little; "   Haggai 1:6

In other words their needs will not be met and their deepest hunger will not be satisfied.

3.) **Physical brokenness.**

Sickness and ill health follows where there has been a disobedience and where financial barrenness is manifest.

4.) Social degradation.

God said to them in Haggai 1:6 *"none will be warm"*. They will wear clothes and not be warm in other words, they will be embarrassed, exposed and put to shame. Social degradation becomes the portion of a person going through a period of financial barrenness.

5.) Economic wastage.

Saddled with unnecessary bills, contingencies and indulgences; the money held back from God is now used in things that do not profit the person who earned the money.

6.) Hyper inflation.

The nation, people or families who refuse to honour God find things inflated and often out of purse.

7.) Shattered dreams; lost hopes.

So God says *"They will look for much but indeed, it will come to little"*.

Their dreams do not match the realities of experience neither are the hopes of a financially barren person in agreement with his experience.

8.) Domestic problems.

Consequently, with the inability to provide, serious argument follows in marriage. A greater percent of family trouble of the modern man is centred around finance. Where the family has leant to honour the lord first, He provides them contentment followed by other supplies.

9.) **Short lived victories.** If they had any breakthrough at all, the heavens again withhold the dew.

10.) Perpetual lack.

"And the earth withholds and refuses to send its blessings upon them ."

11.) Withdrawal of God's approval.

Haggai 1:10 - *"Therefore the heavens above you will withhold the dew and the earth withholds its fruits."*

12.) Absence of divine blessing.

The heavens withholding its dew, this is symbolic of a lack of spiritual freshness or a touch from heaven.

13.) **Divine judgement.**

Consequently, everything is withheld and things dry up.

14.) **Divine sanctions.**

> *"For I called for a drought on the land and the mountains, on the grain and the new wine and the oil, on whatever the ground brings forth, on men, on livestock and on all the labour of you hands." Haggai 1:11*

With divine sanction in the life of a person who is financially barren, things go wrong in five areas as mentioned in this verse.

- It talks of the grain which stands for a sanction on their labour.
- It talks of new wine which is no joy.
- The oil means no anointing.
- The cattle means bad investments and bad returns.
- The labour of the hands means the absence of physical health.

15.) **Barely surviving scanty crops.**

In other words, it becomes tough for a person who

is experiencing financial barrenness to survive because God said that their crops will by scanty.

> *"Therefore the heaven over you is stayed from dew, and the earth is stayed from her fruit."* Haggai 1:10

16.) **Poor returns and depleted savings.**

According to chapter 2 verse 19, *"for all their sowing, they reap very little"*.

17.) **Economic ruin.**

> *"For I called for a drought on the land and the mountains, on the grain and the new wine and the oil, on whatever the ground brings forth, on men, on livestock and on all the labour of you hands."* Haggai 1:11

Lack of favour will lead to economic ruin.

God never leaves His people with a prophetic word of destruction rather He gives a final word of breakthrough. So, God calls them to the conditions for curing financial barrenness.

CURE FOR FINANCIAL BARRENNESS

1.) God demands repentance.

"Thus saith the LORD of hosts; Consider your ways."
Haggai 1:7

2.) God deserves obedience.

*"Then Zerubbabel the son of Shealtiel, and Joshua
the son of Josedech, the high priest with all the
remnant of the people, obeyed the voice of the LORD
their God, and the words of Haggai the prophet, as
the Lord their God had sent him, and the people did
fear before the LORD." Haggai 1:12*

3.) God requires reverence.

*"Then Zerubbabel the son of Shealtiel, and Joshua
the son of Josedech, the high priest with all the
remnant of the people, obeyed the voice of the LORD
their God, and the words of Haggai the prophet, as
the Lord their God had sent him, and the people did
fear before the LORD." Haggai 1:12*

4.) We must learn to receive God's instruction and do what He said.

Haggai came back after the seventh month with a word from the Lord. Do you have a word from the Lord? Apart from the preached messages, we must look to the scriptures for the final say and do what the word of God says not what economics dictates to us. The tithe must not be given only in moments of convenience but to recognise that it is a command of God.

5.) **Be expectant.**

> *"Who is left among you that saw this house in her first glory? And how do ye see it now? Is it not in your eyes in comparison of it as nothing?" Haggai 2:3*

6.) **Be strong.**

> *"Yet now be strong, O Zerubbabel, saith the Lord; and be strong, O Joshua, son of Josedech, the high priest; and be strong, all ye people of the land, saith the* LORD*, and work: for I am with you, saith the* LORD *of hosts:" Haggai 2:4*

7.) **Be led of the Lord.**

Your circumstance should not lead you, also not what friends say. If ones spouse is experiencing difficulty in giving faithfully to the Lord, remember that submission is only as to the Lord. If anything is contrary to the mind of God, God's word takes priority position.

> *"Yet now be strong, O Zerubbabel, saith the Lord; and be strong, O Joshua, son of Josedech, the high priest; and be strong, all ye people of the land, saith the LORD, and work: for I am with you, saith the LORD of hosts:"* Haggai 2:4

8.) **Be bold.**

> *"According to the word that I covenanted with you when you came out of Egypt, so my spirit remains with you, do not fear."* Haggai 2:5

Fear is a thief of the blessing of God, fear will seize the breath in your spirit and make you panic. Fear will stop you from maximising and reaching your highest fulfilment. Remember, God wants you to prosper and no devil can stop you. When you repent, walk in obedience and revere God. The result will be:

1.) **A divine visitation.**

> *"And I will shake all nations, and the desire of all nations shall come: and I will fill this house with glory, saith the LORD of host."* Haggai 2:7

2.) **Glory will be restored back into you life**.

> *"And I will shake all nations, and the desire of all nations shall come: and I will fill this house with glory, saith the LORD of hosts." Haggai 2:7*

Nothing is as tough as a life without glory. Nothing is as empty as a life that does not know glory.

3.) **Financial breakthrough.**

> *"The silver is mine, and the gold is mine, saith the LORD of hosts." Haggai 2:8*

God says that all silver and gold belongs to Him, do not let the devil lie to you and talk you out of your blessing. Satan owns nothing. God made the silver and the gold when He laid the foundation of the earth. We are yet to come into the greatest blessings God has for His people because they are the ones He will use for the propagation of His word in these last days.

4.) **There will be abundant peace.**

> *"The glory of this latter house shall be greater than of the former, saith the LORD of hosts: and in this place will I give peace, saith the LORD of hosts." Haggai 2:9*

5.) **Continuous blessing.**

Chapter 7

PRAYER POINTS

1.) Thank the Lord because He always causes us to have victory in the Lord Jesus Christ.

2.) Give Him praise because He is faithful to keep His promises at all times.

3.) Remember and bless the name of the Lord because no good thing will He withhold from those who trust in Him.

4.) Give God the praise for His promise that those who ask for bread will never be given stone.

5.) Pray that like Rebecca, the Lord will give you breakthrough beyond your expectation in the name of Jesus.

6.) Confess by faith to the face of barrenness that the Lord will bless you with twins. Genesis 38:27

7.) Pray that the Lord will bless the union of the barren person you know as they meet with their spouse in the name of the Lord.

8.) Confess by faith that contrary to the words of experts that the Lord will breakthrough and supply wherever the sperm count has been low, in the name of Jesus.

9.) Pray that the Lord will turn every mockery of your condition to a stepping stone and a greater testimony.

10.) Bless the name of the lord because He will cause you to experience the travail of a pregnant woman.

11.) Confess by faith that you shall experience labour and shall bring forth a living child in the name of Jesus.

12.) Pray that the Lord will make the time of your labour to be comfortable to the glory of His name.

13.) Reject hard labour and prolonged travail in the name of the Lord.

14.) Come against every demonic force that would cause you to lose your child in the name of Jesus.

15.) Confess by faith that the Lord gave you your womb and you will use it to carry your own child in the name of the Lord.

16.) By faith begin to declare the kind of men and women that will be raised in your house in the name of Jesus.

17.) Give God praise for the number of boys and girls he will bless your life with.

18.) Thank the Lord for changing your song to that of a woman whose home is full of children.

19.) Praise the name of the Lord because He has given you a reason to burst into singing as He blesses you with the blessing of the womb.

20.) Give God praise because your testimony changes from *"her who had none"* to *"the one whose house full of children"*.

21.) Boldly declare that your tent shall be enlarged by the reason of the increase of your fruitfulness.

22.) In the realm of the spirit, tear away every wall of limitation that the enemy tries to put around your home.

23.) Thank the Lord because your children shall possess their possession.

24.) By faith begin to pray and claim the blessings that belong to your children in advance, in the name of Jesus.

25.) Boldly declare that one day, you shall be called *"the mother of the children of promise"*.

26.) Take authority over every manifestation of barrenness and declare that you come out of it in the name of Jesus.

27.) Boldly declare according to the word of God, you shall give birth even before labour.

28.) Praise the name of the Lord because before there is pain, you shall deliver your child.

29.) Pray that according to God's word that the children He has for you in His plan will come into you life in the name of Jesus.

30.) Command that every womb that is shut be opened in the name of Jesus.

31.) Thank the Lord because He shall bring to pass the time of birth and the time of delivery in the name of Jesus.

32.) Pray that the Lord will turn around every pain and shame of delay into a reason for a greater testimony.

33.) Reject premature birth in the name of Jesus.

34.) Come against every panic attack that could arise during child birth in Jesus name.

35.) Pray against untimely death, in the family in the name Jesus.

36.) Thank the Lord because you shall not carry any pregnancy in vain for the Lord Himself shall grant you safe delivery in the name of Jesus.

37.) Pray that the Lord will cause the people who prayed with you to rejoice with you also at the birth of your child.

38.) Ask the Lord to turn the pain of those who

have had a delay after the first child to a testimony, in the name of Jesus.

39.) Pray that the period of your long wait and delay will be fully rewarded in Jesus Name.

40.) Give God praise because the glory of the Lord shall rise upon you and all eyes shall see it as He blesses you with the fruit of the labour.

41.) Reject the spirit of fear and receive the peace of God during labour, in the name of Jesus.

42.) Give God praise because He will cause you to experience pregnancy and He shall also give you a safe delivery in the name of Jesus.

43.) Pray that the Lord will turn the evil prediction of experts to nothing, in the name of Jesus.

44.) Take authority over every evil spell or satanic hindrance to your breakthrough in child birth.

45.) Thank the Lord for destroying principalities and powers that are a hindrance to your receiving your blessing of the fruit of the womb, in the name of the Lord.

46.) By faith confess that you receive the breakthrough of child birth and that the world will rejoice with you in the name of the Lord.

47.) Pray for the peace of God in your child birth, in the name of Jesus.

48.) Declare by faith as a man who is trusting God for the fruit of the womb that your loins are full of children.

49.) Pray that every negative report concerning your partner will turn to positive, in the name of Jesus.

50.) Thank the Lord because he is about to turn your delay into a testimony.

51.) Pray that your period of waiting will turn around quickly to breakthrough in the name of Jesus.

52.) Receive by faith all the children that God has for you in the realm of the spirit.

53.) Come against every weapon the enemy has been using against you becoming pregnant.

54.) Reach forth into the spirit realm and tear down

every hindrance to your pregnancy in the name of Jesus.

55.) Release the blessing of child birth which God has for you in the realm of the spirit, in the name of Jesus.

56.) Destroy every cage used and built around your blessing by the enemy and receive by faith the breakthrough of fruit bearing.

57.) Ask the Lord to give you a testimony that will cause those who knew you as *"barren"* to now know you as *"the mother of children".*

58.) Boldly declare that by reason of God's favour, you shall become a woman whom *"her children arise up, and call her blessed".*

59.) Declare by faith that your time of child birth shall not be the time of trouble but the time of testimony in the name of the Lord.

60.) Bless the name of the Lord because those whom you have rejoiced with for their own child birth shall rejoice with you.

61.) Declare by faith that the children the Lord shall

bless you with shall be full of wisdom and they will be blessed and highly favoured.

62.) Pray against any plans of the enemy to hurt your children.

63.) Declare by faith that the spirit of the Lord protects you from post natal depression.

64.) Thank the Lord in advance for the blessing of fruit bearing; for what He gives is without sorrow.

65.) Boldly reject miscarriage in the name of Jesus.

66.) Thank the Lord by faith because He has not given you dry breasts but breasts to feed your own children in the name of Jesus.

67.) Declare by faith that your dryness, barrenness and fruitlessness shall turn into testimony in the name of the Lord.

68.) Make a vow to the Lord of what you children will do to the glory of God in His vineyard.

69.) Thank the Lord because He will give your children that are arrows in the hand of the Lord, for the destruction of the work of the enemy.

70.) Confess by faith that your house shall be full of children male and female that bring glory to the name of the Lord.

71.) Thank the Lord for changing your fruitlessness to fruit bearing.

72.) Boldly declare that after your breakthrough in child birth, you will go from victory to victory and have more children as you desire in the name of Jesus.

73.) Pray in advance that your children will not be evil but children of promise and blessing.

74.) Protect yourself with the blood of Jesus against phantom pregnancy.

75.) Boldly declare that every attempt to replace the fruit of the womb in you with emptiness shall not stand in the name of Jesus.

76.) Declare by faith that God who brings you to the state of pregnancy shall also bring you to a safe delivery to the glory of His name, in the name of Jesus.

77.) Thank the Lord in advance because the children

He shall give you shall not be called trouble or mischief, but sources of victory and testimony in the land.

78.) Receive the grace by faith to walk in truthfulness and not deceit as you trust in the Lord for the fruit of the womb in the name of Jesus.

79.) Pray that every attempt of the enemy to use the delay in child bearing to tear your marriage apart will not work in Jesus name.

80.) Bind every attempt of satan to use family members to cause confusion in you marriage in the name of the Lord.

81.) Declare by faith that the mistakes of the past will not hinder you from the blessing of the future in the name of Jesus.

82.) Reach forth into the realm of the spirit and take boldly that which belongs to you regarding child bearing in the name of Jesus.

83.) Boldly declare in advance that just as you were given birth to, you shall also bear the fruit of your womb.

84.) Rejoice in the Lord in advance because not only would you see the fruit of the womb, you shall see your grand children.

85.) Thank the Lord for forgiving you of all your sexual sins in the past in the name of Jesus.

86.) Confess by faith that every mistake in the area of abortion will not stop you from receiving the blessing that God has in the future in the name of Jesus.

87.) Thank the Lord because for all you shame, He will give you testimony and joy and make you the mother of children.

88.) Receive total healing by faith for every veneral disease that may hinder you from becoming pregnant in the name of Jesus.

89.) Curse the root of fibroid, cyst and every strange growth in your body in the name of our Lord Jesus.

90.) Declare by faith that your hormones and every part of your body *'agrees'* with pregnancy in the name of the Lord.

91.) Thank God because no defilement of the past

shall stop you from bearing and holding your babies in the name of Jesus.

92.) Rejoice in the Lord by faith because, as He makes you to be pregnant, you shall enjoy the victory in the name of Jesus.

93.) Thank the Lord for the supernatural intervention that will result in your pregnancy in the name of Jesus.

94.) Give God praise because He will give you a visitation that will result in the testimony of childbirth.

95.) Give God praise because like Zechariah, the breakthrough God will give to your wife will be marvellous.

96.) Pray boldly that like Elizabeth, even in you old age you shall still give birth to children in Jesus name.

97.) Reject unbelief, and doubts about the favour of the Lord and the blessing of childbirth.

98.) Pray that the Lord will turn the counsel and the opinion of experts concerning your health to nought.

99.) Rejoice in the Lord because He has taken away your reproach and regret and has turned them to a time of testimony.

100.) Pray boldly that you who was called *"barren"* shall now be called *"blessed"*.

 101.) Give God praise because according to His word, nothing shall be impossible.

102.) Lay hand on your body and begin to declare that it shall be a carrier of the blessing of God.

103.) Declare boldly into your life that you shall be called *"the blessed of the Lord in the area of fruit bearing"*.

104.) Declare that like Sarah, you shall still bear fruit in old age.

105.) Give God praise because He is the faithful judge and He would favour you with the blessing of the fruit of the womb.

 106.) Pray for the strength to conceive even if you have been told it is not possible. *or unlikely*

107.) Come against every genetic disorder in your family which has caused your delay in the name of Jesus.

108.) Destroy every curse of barrenness in your family to the third and fourth generation in the name of Jesus.

109.) Boldly declare that the baby in you shall not be still born but full of life in the name of Jesus.

110.) Pray against every declaration of *"dead of arrival"* and declare that you shall have a living child on delivery in Jesus name.

111.) Lay your hand on yourself and declare that the baby in you shall not be aborted but shall be full of life and shall have a testimony.

112.) Thank the Lord because you shall carry your baby to the fullness of time and all eyes shall see what the Lord has done.

113.) Proclaim your freedom from all biological complications in the name of the Lord.

114.) Prophecy that what has been called a small womb in you life shall become big enough to carry your pregnancy.

115.) Cancel every plan of the enemy to cause genetic disorder in the life of children which the Lord shall give you.

116.) Cover your future with the blood so that no form of deformity shall be found in the name of the Lord.

117.) Speak against every attempt of the enemy to cause sickness and disease in the body of your children which the Lord shall give you in Jesus name.

118.) Boldly declare your freedom from every curse of barrenness in you family to the third and forth generation.

119.) Raise your voice and plead to the Lord concerning your wife that the Lord will give her a breakthrough in child bearing.

120.) Lay your hand of faith on you wife and pronounce conception into her life in the name of Jesus.

121.) Agree as a couple and declare yourselves free of every curse of barrenness that may have been placed on you.

122.) Agree as a couple and declare yourselves free from every genetic and generational curse you may have inherited that may have caused delay in fruit bearing.

123.) Boldly declare that the enemy shall not abort the visions which the Lord has given you.

124.) Take authority over every delay in your vision and declare your total victory in the name of Jesus.

125.) Rejoice in the Lord because your idea shall not be still born.

126.) Give God praise because there shall not be premature birth with the ideas God has given you but you vision shall come to pass according to the time of life.

127.) Refuse and reject every attempt of the enemy to take your life while in the process of childbirth.

128.) Confess by faith that you shall not experience breech birth or any other complications in Jesus name.

129.) Pray that your affliction of barrenness will be turned around to childbirth.

130.) If you suffer from rejection, ask the Lord to intervene in your situation in the name of Jesus.

131.) Thank the Lord because like Leah, He will turn your persecution to praise and your shame to testimony.

132.) Pray that the time of the birth of your children shall be a time of bonding and love in your family.

133.) Stand on the word of God that according to Exodus 23:26, none shall be barren in you house.

134.) Boldly declare that the days of your pregnancy and delivery shall be fulfilled.

135.) Thank the Lord for taking away every form of sickness and disease causing a hindrance to child birth in your family.

136.) Stand on the promise of the Lord that there shall be no barren in you house whether male or female.

137.) Prophesy into everything that pertains to you life, work, home and church that no unfruitfulness follows you in Jesus name.

138.) Confess by faith that the children that the Lord

shall give you will be a deliverer like Samson.

139.) Make a vow to the Lord of what you shall do when the Lord opens the door and blesses you with your children.

140.) Thank God for turning the provocation of the enemy to the source of strength for you as you wait on the Lord for your child.

141.) Pray that the *"one"* child that the Lord will give you shall equal *"seven"* of those who have not trusted in Him.

142.) Give God praise and thank Him because you know that you delay does not mean a denial; you shall yet have the miracle of you childbirth.

143.) Pray for all those who have mocked you and provoked you like Penninah that they shall not die but be alive to see the goodness of God in you.

144.) Take authority and destroy the work of demon spirits that take advantage of barren wombs. Job 24:21

145.) Reject every lie of satan that says your state of barrenness is a punishment from God and thank God for healing you.

146.) Stand on the word of God and declare the number of children you desire. If you want twins or more, the Lord will grant your desire. Songs of Solomon 4:2.

147.) Bless the name of the Lord because none shall be barren in your family in the name of Jesus.

148.) Come against the spirit of barrenness that plagues you local church and declare it a fruitful church in Jesus name.

149.) Plead the blood of Jesus against the spirit that aborts you plans and vision in the name of the Lord.

150.) Plead the blood of Jesus against the spirit that aborts the vision of your family in the name of Jesus.

151.) Give God praise because He will not withhold any good thing from your family in the name of the Lord.

152.) Pray that the testimony of your success will become a source of challenge and encouragement to other people.

153.) Ask the Lord to help you overcome the

thought that your breakthrough is too late.

154.) Reject and refuse every image, teaching, suggestion, voice or expert who says God cannot do it in your life.

155.) Bless the name of the Lord because faithful is he who has promised who also will do it in your life.

156.) Pray that the Lord will turn your womb to the source of life.

157.) Declare that according to II Kings 2:21, there shall be no more death or barrenness in everything that pertains to your life.

158.) Boldly speak life into everything that pertains to your life which has a manifestation of barrenness and call fruitfulness into it.

159.) Pray that the fruits of self-control and godliness that changes barrenness to fruitfulness will be manifest in you life.

160.) Release the power of the Holy Spirit to destroy every root of unfruitfulness in every area of your life in the name of the Lord.

161.) Give God praise because fruitfulness will follow your ministry and work in the vineyard of the Lord.

162.) Plead the blood of Jesus against the spirit of doubt attacking the blessing and fruitfulness God is bringing to you.

163.) Pray for everyone you know who is experiencing delay after previous childbirth that God will give them breakthrough in the name of the Lord.

164.) Ask the Lord to give you the children that will be a source of joy and not heart break.

165.) Give God praise because of His promise to fill your quiver with blessed children.

166.) Possess the future of your coming children and declare your vision for them in the name of Jesus.

167.) Declare by faith that no weapon formed against your children will prosper in the name of the Lord.

168.) Cancel every evil pronouncement made into your life that has caused barrenness in the name of the Lord.

169.) Thank the Lord for forgiving you of any sin that could cause delay and blockage in the name of Jesus.

170.) Plead the blood of Jesus against every kind of gynaecological problem, for example tube blockage in the name of the Lord.

171.) Stand on the word of God and declare that God will turn your house to a home full of children.

172.) Pray fervently that the Lord will use the testimony of the divine turnaround in your situation to bring souls to Christ.

173.) Pray that the Lord will open the door of favour for you and other friends trusting Him for the fruit of the womb.

174.) Give God praise because you shall be known and call *"the joyful mother of children"*.

175.) Thank the Lord because like Sarah, He will make you laugh again by reason of fruitfulness.

176.) Take authority over every failure of the ovary and declare that it shall reach maturity in Jesus name.

178.) Pray that every deformity inherited from birth, which is affecting your reproduction, will be healed of the Lord.

179.) Receive God's healing from cysts and every growth that is affecting the regular production of hormones in your body.

180.) Pray that every ovulatory disorder in your body as a woman will be healed of the Lord and God will give you a testimony in Jesus name.

181.) Receive healing from the Lord for all other things, which you might not know are in your body that are causing a hindrance.

182.) Pray that excessive weight loss or gain causing barrenness will stop in the name of Jesus.

183.) Pray that every blockage of the ovary will be healed of the Lord in Jesus name.

184.) Take authority over every kind of infection that is causing a delay in your life.

185.) Lay your hand on you stomach and declare that every abnormality in the womb will be corrected.

186.) Pray that the shape, positioning and other things of the womb will be regulated by the power of God.

187.) Take authority over every form of antibody that is destroying the health of your body and delaying productivity in the name of Jesus.

188.) Pray that every male infertility will be corrected and healing will follow in Jesus name.

189.) Confess by faith that instead of a low sperm count, you are healed of God and you have an accurate sperm count.

190.) Thank the Lord because he owns your body and you are free from erectile impotence in Jesus name.

191.) Ask the Lord for forgiveness and pray that every sexually transmitted disease affecting the pathway of the sperm will be cleared in Jesus name.

192.) Thank God for healing you from other growths in the body mumps, that can affect your ability to reproduce.

193.) Lay the hand of faith on your children and

begin to declare into their life that every abnormal growth, be corrected of the Lord in Jesus name.

194.) Pray about every operation you have done in the past, which may be hindering you fruitfulness.

195.) Ask the Lord to heal you of every cancerous growth.

196.) Pray against toxic chemicals that are damaging your reproductive organs.

197.) Pray for healing from all the effects of alcohol and drugs in your body system.

198.) Pray that every genetic and generational problem in your life will stop forthwith.

199.) Thank God because you will be healed and will not need the recommended operation.

200.) Confess by faith that you will not go through labour pain without a positive result.

Chapter 8

CONFESSION

I give God Praise because His word is true. His faithfulness is forever. I believe and confess that according to God's word I am fruitful in the name of Jesus. I boldly declare in the face of barrenness that the Lord will bless me with the fruit of the womb. According to His word, my house shall be filled with the blessing of children, for the Lord Himself shall make me the mother of the children of promise.

I believe and confess that God will bring to pass a time of pregnancy, birth and delivery in my life. I reject premature birth or children not carried to full term. I cover my life and baby with the blood of Jesus. I boldly declare that no weapon formed against me prospers and every mouth that rises against me in judgement shall be condemned.

I believe and confess that the spirit of fear has no power over me. I take authority over every spell, or satanic hindrance, which is obstructing my way. I destroy principalities and powers that are a hindrance to receiving my blessing of the fruit of the womb.

I believe and confess that any negative report concerning my partner and I will turn around for good. I boldly declare that every genetic disorder shall be healed of the Lord.

I receive the healing of the Lord, by faith, for my womb, body and for my spouse.

I believe and confess that the children the Lord shall bless me with shall be filled with wisdom and they will be highly favoured. I take authority over sorrow, pain hurt, ungodly children, postnatal depression and every other negative attack. I boldly reject a miscarrying womb in the name of the Lord.

I declare by faith that the dryness, barrenness and fruitfulness shall turn to testimony. My vineyard shall be full of fruitfulness. My barren and arid desert shall become a fruitful garden. The Lord himself shall protect me with His blood against phantom pregnancy.

I boldly declare that the grace of Jesus Christ is enough for me therefore I shall give testimony of His faithfulness in the assembly of His people. I rejoice in the Lord in advance because not only will I hold the fruit of my womb but I shall see my children's children according to God's word.

I take authority over the root of every growth in my body, fibroids, cysts and every strange manifestation. I declare my healing in the name of the Lord. I pray that the Lord will turn the counsel and the opinion of experts concerning my health to nought. I boldly declare that the Lord will bless me in every area, with every blessing of the womb. Today I prophesy that what has been called a "small womb"; "a barren womb" shall become filled with the blessing of the Lord. I will stand in the assembly of God's people and testify of God's faithfulness and goodness in the name of Jesus.

Congratulation, you are going to have a baby!

Chapter 9

TESTIMONIES

Late 1995, during the month of *"total turnaround"*, Pastor Matthew asked us to list at least ten things that we desire to come to pass in 1996. The very first thing on my list was the fruit of the womb, which I had been waiting on God for, for the past seven years.

On one of the Sunday evening services during that month, Pastor ministered and prayed for us concerning the fruit of the womb, we were admonished to take a step of faith, believing that with God all things are possible. I was personally touched by the message and the following morning which was on a Monday, I went to Argos and I bought baby utilities which I immediately anointed, desperately waiting on God to grant my desire.

Several months later, nothing happened and I found myself doubting if anything was going to happen. Then about the same time, my cousin called me and informed me that she was expecting and because I was a bit sceptical about mine, I told her to come and take the baby things I bought earlier. She accepted the offer.

Meanwhile, I had booked an appointment with the Pastor's wife for prayer and we met and prayed together concerning the issue. In the service that followed, Pastor Matthew taught about restoration of wombs and made Deuteronomy 7:14 clearer that God does not like barrenness in His house. Then the Holy Spirit led me to Psalm 50:14 to make a vow in unpleasant times and He will make it come to past for His glorification. I subsequently made a vow to the Lord of a specified amount and I was absolutely glad when I was confirmed pregnant in late 1996. Which meant I did not have to give my cousin the baby things.

Praise God, in 1997, I gave birth to a blessed, highly favoured, beautiful girl. To God be the Glory.

B. A.

MY MIRACLE BABY

For 15 years I tried to have a baby. I tried everything available medically. I did two operations and had three sections of IVF treatments none of which results to a baby.

After my third IVF treatment my husband and I decided we would not go through any more treatment, but continue to see the doctor and hope for a miracle to happen.

We prayed and fasted for another year, nothing happened. Due to the pressure on us and humiliation faced from people, my husband decided we should try another treatment. I insisted I was not going for any more of that treatment, because not only was the treatment painful but emotionally stressful. I told him my God is sufficient for me. God's report is that I will have a baby, because He said there shall be no barren in His house and I believed if He could do it for Sarah and Abraham He will do it for us.

I continued to pray, fast, and hope for miracle to happen. During the month of fasting and praying in December 1996, Jesus showed up in my case. I tested positive that is, (pregnant) in January, that morning from 5 am I praised and thanked God all day for His loving kindness, because He gave us a big gift which no one can give.

The Devil is a liar, when my pregnancy was 18 weeks old, the devil tried and failed. I nearly lost the baby but the Lord took control of everything. I was discharged from the hospital after a week.

At 28 weeks my water broke one morning. I thought I was going to have the baby immediately, but the doctors said the baby could still stay inside for more weeks, as long as I stayed in bed doing nothing. For another week I was in bed resting. While I was in bed I spent most of my time praying, reminding God of all His promises concerning me and my baby, that we would not die but live to declare the glory of God. I prayed to have a safe delivery and healthy baby most of the day. I know that the doctors can only try but the highest doctor (Lord) can do it all. He is able.

To the glory of God, I gave birth to a beautiful, healthy baby girl five days later. Praise God. It was the best day of my life, though I was tired, I felt stronger than ever. We were full of joy that at last we have our own baby.

My baby stayed another seven weeks in hospital because she was born 11 weeks premature and was very small in weight. The seven weeks was hectic and stressful, but the grace of God helped us through it.

I give God the praise, honour and adoration for His miracle in our lives and in the life of our families. He has turned our 'mourning to dancing' and our 'tears to streams of joy'. I pray God in His mercy would bless everyone waiting for one thing or another, especially people waiting for the fruit of the womb. God will renew their faith and bless them with wonderful children. Amen.

Mrs. A.T.

WAITING ON THE LORD

O Give thanks unto the Lord; for He is good, because His mercy endureth forever.

This testimony is about how God answered our prayers for a baby after seven years of waiting and trusting in the Lord. The story is very long with many twists and turns, but I will attempt to summarise the whole story as follows;

1. The Genesis

I met my wife in 1988 and decided to get married on the 24th February 1990 after many months of courtship. We decided to start a family straightaway though we were not quite ready for the responsibility of being parents. My wife and I then prayed together one night about having a successful marriage, God fearing and loving family and also be good parents to our children. After the prayers, we discussed the number of children we would like to have as a family but were unable to complete the discussion because we could not agree on the number of children; either 2 or 3 children.

2. The Waiting

From October 1990 to May 1997, we were trusting the Lord for a baby. We fasted, did a lot of prayers and night vigils, asking and reminding God about His promise that there will never be a barren in His house. During this same period, we had many financial situations and other pressures from friends and the brethren in our previous Church which sometimes took our minds away from the situation and made us come more close to God.

There were diverse temptations but God gave us the strength and courage to withstand them all. Most annoying of all was some friends and Church members questioning my manhood and sexual relationship with my wife; but God gave me the wisdom to deal with them all and to continue to encourage my wife that the Lord is good and righteous and shall answer in His own time.

My wife started buying baby clothes and toys in 1992 in anticipation of having a baby that year. During this time, we have consulted the Doctors and gynaecologists about the situation and all tests proved to be all right. After waiting for another year, we decided to consult a specialist gynaecologist in Harley Street. After the initial consultation with no conclusive results, I calculated the costs of undergoing the full treatment and decided against it.

In September 1993, my wife went for an operation to check her womb et cetera and they found that everything with her reproductive system was in perfect order and functioning perfectly; thank God. Now the problems began, if it was not my wife then it was bound to be me. I was asked to do a semen test, which came back positive. We were then advised to keep on trying. We continued praying and trusting in the Lord because we strongly believed that the God we serve is a living God and He will surely answer us.

We joined KICC in April 1997, I attended my first service at KICC on the 13th April 1997 and my wife joined me a week later. That same month, Pastor Matthew started a preaching on a very unique message titled "Congratulations you are going to have a baby". I felt that message was for us and we claimed it in Jesus name.

3. The Result

The month of May was declared the month of fruitfulness, which happened to fit in well with the preceding messages of Pastor Matthew. During the month of May, God came into time, looked at my family and answered our prayers. Halleluya!

In April, I was asked to do a semen test by the Doctors, since they had tried everything else and failed. When the result came back, I was diagnosed to have a low sperm count. I instantly rejected it and claimed my rightful portion of abundance sperm count in Jesus' Name. In fact, the way I characterised my prayer that day was so funny that my wife could not stop laughing for days.

The Doctors advised us to consider the IVF treatment as a last resort having tried all other sources for 7 years. I rejected the idea and prayed steadfastly during that period. One night while praying, God gave me a word in season, which has been my motto from then - "No man can share the glory of God, ". I repeated that throughout that week and asked my wife to also use it in prayers.

I got all the information about the IVF treatment and studied it carefully. The analysis of all its test and treatment taken were very poor with only 1 in 15 had successful birth and many ended up in other complications and severe health problems. Then, I was more convinced that it was the wrong option and I did not want my wife to have the treatment but she insisted on having the IVF and even offered to pay for it herself.

While we were busy arguing about the matter, God had already done His work in the spiritual realm and waiting for it to be manifested in the physical realm. During one Sunday service in May, while Pastor Matthew was praying, he gave a prophecy that "God has given a child to a couple in the service and it was long overdue" my wife and I claimed it. That same month my wife got pregnant as God had spoken through His minister - glory to God in the highest.

We did not know until 1st July 1997 after a urine test at the local chemist because she was feeling very uncomfortable and always tired. She called the chemist to confirm the test result and she was told it was positive, that she was pregnant! We were both in the car going to a business appointment in Weybridge when she turned to me and said "Emmanuel, it is positive" I was shocked and confused and did not understand what she meant by positive. Amidst the confusion, I decided to call the pharmacist again just to hear him confirm the same thing and he explained the result of the urine test to me. And when he said "yes, she is pregnant", I just could not explain the joy that filled my heart at that moment. I parked my car on the hard shoulder on the M25 to pray and thank the Lord.

The pregnancy went smoothly with no morning sickness, no fear and the spirit of God was upon the baby and mother. In a nutshell, God gave us a beautiful, loving girl on Sunday 1st March 1998. The labour was only three and a half hours to the amazement of the doctors and midwives because when my wife started having contractions, she was still laughing and looking relaxed. The baby came into our lives exactly eight long years after our marriage.

With this big testimony, I want the whole Church to praise the Lord for us because this is a living proof that God answers prayers but His timing might not be the same as ours. God is a master planner, the author and finisher of our faith.

I pray that God in His mercy will hear the prayers of those still waiting on him for the fruit of the womb and will bless them with good children from the throne of grace. God has proven to me that He can bring forth life out of nothing so I pray that He should extend this same joy to other people in similar situations that by this time next year, they shall surely have a child in Jesus' name. Amen

The Lord is good all the time! God bless you

Brother and Sister E. M.

GOD DID IT

My husband and I had been trusting God for the blessing of the fruit of the womb for four years. During those years, we joined KICC in January 1995 and went for counselling and prayer of deliverance. Also, in 1995, we both went for medical check-ups and it was diagnosed that I had a cyst on one of my ovaries. We shared the report with the Pastor of counselling and he prayed for me. To the glory of God, when I went for my next appointment at the hospital, the cyst was not longer on my ovary.

My husband and I were very glad about this news and thought I would get pregnant soon, but another year passed still no pregnancy.

After some months in 1996, I told my husband that I would like to go for another internal check called laparoscopy. Initially, he rejected the idea saying that we should stay focused on God. After much persuasion from me, he gave me the go-ahead and in June 1996, I had a laparoscopy operation carried out under full anaesthetic. The result showed that I had a blocked tube, but before I left the hospital the gynaecologist discussed other alternatives of conception with me and said if we were that desperate we could consider IVF. I passed the information to my husband and he said I should forget about IV fertilisation and other check-ups as God will cause us to have a breakthrough in His own time.

We discussed the issue of fruit of the womb with our Pastor. I told him all we have done medically and he replied by reading out a statement on a tracts which stated "God Did It". He said it was prophetic and that I should be at peace within myself for God will answer us. Another year went by still no sign of pregnancy, in April 1997 I raised the issue of IVF with my husband which he still refused flatly. I tried to make him understand that IVF was not a bad option and even begged him but he still refused. This made me very sad and there was tension in our house. After some days, my husband told me to go ahead with the with the IVF process (just to make me happy).

Immediately I contacted our family Doctor who referred me to the hospital and the hospital was to contact us at a later date.

When we got to the church that evening, the Senior Pastor started a teaching series that evening titled "Congratulations, you are going to have a baby".

He taught based on eight different women in the bible that waited on the Lord for a baby. He described each situation to be unique and encouraged everyone waiting on the Lord for a blessing of the fruit of the womb to trust God. I felt encouraged by the sermon but the issue of IVF still came back to my mind. The month of May 1997 was declared the month of fruitfulness. On Sunday 18 May 1997 during the evening service the Senior Pastor called me out and gave me a prophetic word.

Meanwhile I was still waiting for the hospital to reply us. The letter finally came at the end of May 1997 with its contents being very discouraging. Amongst other conditions, we were told that it would take approximately four years for us to get on the waiting list for the IVF programme. I tried again to persuade my husband that we could use a private hospital, as usual he sail he was not going to spend any money for private treatment. At this point, I dropped the idea of IVF and started going to the gymnasium in order to occupy my mind, without realising that while I was waiting for the hospital to contact us, I had already conceived.

I knew I was pregnant at the end of June 1997 when it occurred to me that I did not keep records of my monthly period for May 1997. This prompted me to buy a pregnancy kit which after using, proved positive. I conceived in May 1997 (Month of Fruitfulness) and our precious baby girl was born in February 1998 (Month of Double Honours) three days to my birthday.

God's ways are not our ways, to Him be all the Glory, Honour and Praise.

M.O.

THE LORD GAVE ME MY HEALING

In April 1993, we gave birth to our precious son in the United States by caesarean section and I suffered from what was referred to as a minor infection afterwards. This was treated and the extent of any damaged was not known.

By 1995, my husband and I began trusting God for another child. When nothing seemed to be happening, we went to the doctor and I was put on the waiting list.

In July 1996, I underwent a private medical investigation in America, to find out why I was not conceiving. The result showed a possibility of a blocked fallopian tube. I returned to England where I was on a waiting list to see a specialist. In March 1997 I was scheduled for a 'laproscopy' surgery (to view the inside of my uterus). The doctor (at Homerton Hospital) told my husband and I that both fallopian tubes were damaged as a result of an infection which occurred 4 years ago after undergoing a caesarean section childbirth.

By March 1997, after the laproscopy surgery, the doctor told my husband and I that it would be impossible for me to conceive any child naturally, that the only solution will be by IVF and not even tubal surgery can correct the damage.

We did not give up hope instead we kept praying more fervently. We now have a difficult decision to make to go for the IVF treatment or not. After the June 1997 prayer and fasting, we opted for the IVF treatment. In July 1997, as we were on our way for the egg collection, I was reading a book by Benny Hinn. "THIS IS YOUR DAY FOR A MIRACLE". To my surprise the first page I opened was titled "Julie Day". I showed it to my husband who was driving us to the hospital. We both said without any doubt that we would share the miracle on that very story.

The transplant was successful and we were told to wait till 4th August 1997 to know if I was pregnant or not. Then came that faithful 4th August 1997 morning, I discovered that I was bleeding. The IVF therefore was unsuccessful. My husband was very supportive all through this period. He said to me that we had gone our own way; mans' way. It was now time for spiritual warfare. My entire household registered for the August 1997 Gathering of Champions' School of miracles, signs and wonders.

During this conference, attending this school truly fired up our spirit and we became prayer warriors.

Then came the first week of September, Pastor Matthew called out all those who were believing God for the fruit of the womb and he laid hands on every one of us. Afterwards, a woman was called out to give her testimony. She testified to the miracle of God. She has just had a baby after waiting for many years.

As I prayed during that very service, a voice said to me to make an offering of thanksgiving. I had no more money in my purse. I reached out to my husband and I asked him for whatever he had in his wallet. I made the Lord a thanksgiving offering. A month later, October I discovered that I was pregnant. To God be the glory. He opened up my tubes and made possible what man said was impossible, my baby is now due in June 1998 in Jesus Name. The Lord is my healer.

J. D.

* Since receiving this testimony, J.D. had a baby boy. The second miracle was that it was conceived in a ruptured tube. The statement of the Doctor who delivered her was " How the h... did you get pregnant".

Congratulation, you are going to have a baby!

OTHER PRODUCTS BY THE AUTHOR

TAPE PACKS:

Title	Code	Amount	Quantity	Price
2 TAPE PACKS				
Dangers Of Indebtedness	2TP001	£6:00		
Releasing His Glory	2TP002	£6:00		
Breaking The Bondage Of The Mind	2TP003	£6:00		
Overcoming The Attacks Of The Enemy	2TP004	£6:00		
Single Spot	2TP005	£6:00		
Breaking Generational Curses	2TP006	£6:00		
The Power For The Miraculous	2TP007	£6:00		
Overcoming Your Worst Storms	2TP008	£6:00		
Living In Total Victory	2TP009	£6:00		
The Eagle Believer	2TP010	£6:00		
Dealing With Difficult People	2TP011	£6:00		
Marks Of Total Victory	2TP012	£6:00		
Winning In The Family	2TP013	£6:00		
Provoking God For A Turnaround	2TP014	£6:00		
Praying For A Turnaround	2TP015	£6:00		
Singles Time Out	2TP016	£6:00		
Fasting And Praying	2TP017	£6:00		
Preparing Yourself For Victory	2TP018	£6:00		
Secrets Of Abundance	2TP019	£6:00		
What To Do At The Bus Stop Called Lion Den	2TP020	£6:00		
Living Wise In The Seasons Of Life	2TP021	£6:00		
The Happiest People On Earth	2TP022	£6:00		
From Pit To Palace	2TP023	£6:00		
The Journey Of Faith	2TP024	£6:00		
Turning Your Trials To Triumph	2TP025	£6:00		
The Realm Of The Spirit	2TP026	£6:00		
3 TAPE PACKS				
Excellence In Life & Ministry	3TP027	£9:00		
The Manifestation Of Divine Success	3TP028	£9:00		
The Enemies Of The Eagle Believer	3TP029	£9:00		
Overcoming Financial Setbacks	3TP030	£9:00		
The Happy Attitudes	3TP031	£9:00		
Supernatural Living	3TP032	£9:00		

Sub_Total _____

*Shipping _____

Total _____

Congratulation, you are going to have a baby!

Title	Code	Amount	Quantity	Price
Kingdom Authority	3TP033	£9:00		
Financial Prosperity	3TP034	£9:00		
Secrets Of Increase	3TP035	£9:00		
The Devil Is A Liar	3TP036	£9:00		
Evidence For Miracle Living	3TP037	£9:00		
Mandate Of A Champion	3TP038	£9:00		
Marks Of A Champion	3TP039	£9:00		
Songs Of A Champion	3TP040	£9:00		
Leaving Yesterdays Behind	3TP041	£9:00		
Principle Of Divine Increase	3TP042	£9:00		
Devil Dirty Dozen	3TP043	£9:00		
Fulfilling Your Destiny	3TP044	£9:00		
Congrats! You Are Going To Have A Baby	3TP045	£9:00		
The Devil's Dirty Dozen	3TP046	£9:00		
4 TAPE PACKS				
The Road To Success - Volume 1	4TP047a	£12:00		
The Road To Success - Volume 2	4TP047b	£12:00		
The Road To Success - Volume 3	4TP047c	£12:00		
The Road To Success - Volume 4	4TP047d	£12:00		
The Road To Success - Volume 5	4TP047e	£12:00		
The Road To Success - Volume 6	4TP047f	£12:00		
The Road To Success - Volume 7	4TP047g	£12:00		
The Road To Success - Volume 8	4TP047h	£12:00		
The Road To Success - Volume 9	4TP047i	£12:00		
The Road To Success - Volume 10	4TP047j	£12:00		
The Road To Success - Volume 11	4TP047k	£12:00		
The Road To Success - Volume 12	4TP047l	£12:00		
Get Rid Of That Mess	4TP048	£12:00		
Living At The Gate Of Praise	4TP049	£12:00		
Prayer	4TP050	£12:00		
The Making Of A Winner	4TP051	£12:00		
Harvest	4TP052	£12:00		
Miracles	4TP053	£12:00		
Preparing The Champions	4TP054	£12:00		
Divine Visitation	4TP055	£12:00		
Fruitfulness	4TP056	£12:00		
The Struggle Is Over	4TP057	£12:00		
Open Heavens	4TP058	£12:00		
Divine Healing	4TP059	£12:00		
People Just Like Us	4TP060	£12:00		
The Anointing	4TP061	£12:00		

Sub_Total _____
*Shipping _____
Total _____

122

Title	Code	Amount	Quantity	Price
5 TAPE PACKS				
Operating In Financial Excellence	5TP062	£15:00		
Debt Free Living	5TP063	£15:00		
101 Truths About The Holy Spirit	5TP064	£15:00		
6 Tape Packs				
It's Not Over Till'it Is Over	6TP065	£18:00		
The Beginning Of The End	6TP066	£18:00		
The Benefits Of The Name Jesus	6TP067	£18:00		
What On Earth Have You Been Saying?	6TP068	£18:00		
Fasting And Prayer	6TP069	£18:00		
8 TAPE PACKS				
120 Facts About Divine Healing	8TP070	£24:00		
8 Days Of The Anointing	8TP071	£24:00		
10 TAPE PACKS				
Man Of Honour	10TP072	£30:00		
10 Sign Post To Success	10TP073	£30:00		
Marriage Matters Volume 1	10TP074	£30:00		
Marriage Matters Volume 2	10TP075	£30:00		
13 TAPE PACKS				
Quality Christain Living	13TP076	£36:00		
BOOKS:				
It's Not Over 'till it's Over	BK001	£5:95		
The Power Of Positive Prayer	BK002	£9:95		
The Power Of Positive Prayer Volume 2	BK003	£10:00		
The Power Of Positive Prayer Volume 3	BK004	£10:00		
The Power Of Positive Confession 1	BK005	£5:00		
The Power Of Positive Confession Volume 2	BK006	£8:00		
101 Truths About Your Best Friend The Holy Spirit	BK007	£3:50		
101 Truths About Prayer & Fasting	BK008	£3:50		
101 Truths About Divine Success	BK009	£3:50		
Keeping Your Dreams Alive	BK010	£2:50		
The Making Of Champions	BK011	£4:99		
Take A Giant Leap	BK012	£2:50		
Tongues Of Fire	BK013	£2:50		
Warriors Of Righteousness	BK014	£4:95		

Sub_Total _____

*Shipping _____

Total _____

SINGLE TAPES:

Title	Code	Amount	Quantity	Price
The Beginning Of The End (Rapture)	ST001	£3:00		
The Believer's Authority	ST002	£3:00		
The Benefits Of Salvation	ST003	£3:00		
The Blood Of His Covenant	ST004	£3:00		
The Call To Witness	ST005	£3:00		
The Gifts Of The Holy Spirit	ST006	£3:00		
The Glory And Manifest Power Of God	ST007	£3:00		
The God Kind Of Faith	ST008	£3:00		
The God Kind Of Life	ST009	£3:00		
The God Kind Of Love	ST010	£3:00		
The Greatest Name - Jesus	ST011	£3:00		
The Happy Attitudes: I Need Help	ST012	£3:00		
The Holy Ghost Visitation	ST013	£3:00		
The Holy Spirit: Baptism, In-Filling & Blessings	ST014	£3:00		
The Importance Of Living A Spirit-Led Life	ST015	£3:00		
The Joy Of The Lord	ST016	£3:00		
The Law Of Prayer	ST017	£3:00		
The Making Of A Champion	ST018	£3:00		
The Making Of A Winner: "Fighting To Recover All"	ST019	£3:00		
The Manifest Blessings Of Divine Visitation	ST020	£3:00		
The Marks Of Maturity	ST021	£3:00		
The Ministry Of The Holy Spirit	ST022	£3:00		
The Miracle Of Inner Transformation	ST023	£3:00		
The Miracle Of Seed Faith	ST024	£3:00		
The Order Of Breaking Of Bread	ST025	£3:00		
The Pathway To Power	ST026	£3:00		
The Person Of The Holy Spirit	ST027	£3:00		
The Power Of Attorney	ST028	£3:00		
The Power Of Heaven Bound Prayer	ST029	£3:00		
The Power Of The Name Of Jesus	ST030	£3:00		
The Practice Of Intercession	ST031	£3:00		
The Price Of Spiritual Greatness	ST032	£3:00		
The Principles Of Seed Faith	ST033	£3:00		
The Prison Gates Are Open	ST034	£3:00		
The Reality Of Spiritual Warfare	ST035	£3:00		
The Reason To Praise The Lord	ST036	£3:00		
The Release Of The Glory Of God	ST037	£3:00		
The Ressurector	ST038	£3:00		
The Rivers Of God	ST039	£3:00		

Sub_Total _____

*Shipping _____

Total _____

Title	Code	Amount	Quantity	Price
The Role Played By The Family	ST040	£3:00		
The Sacrifice Of Praise	ST041	£3:00		
The Seven Wonders Of Jesus	ST042	£3:00		
The Shout Of Victory	ST043	£3:00		
The Songs Of Champions	ST044	£3:00		
The Sound Of Triumph	ST045	£3:00		
The Spirit Of Excellence	ST046	£3:00		
The Sure Word Of God	ST047	£3:00		
The Twelve D's Of Destiny	ST048	£3:00		
The Unveiling Of Jesus	ST049	£3:00		
The Visitation Of The Lord	ST050	£3:00		
The Word Of God	ST051	£3:00		
The Wrong Man At The Right Place	ST052	£3:00		
There Is A Strong Man In Me	ST053	£3:00		
Total Victory (Finishing Well)	ST054	£3:00		
Trial To Triumph	ST055	£3:00		
Turning Your Trials To Triumph	ST056	£3:00		
Unity In The Body Of Christ	ST057	£3:00		
Victory Over Setbacks	ST058	£3:00		
Walking In Love - How To Fix Broken Relationship	ST059	£3:00		
Walking With The Holy Spirit	ST060	£3:00		
Watchnite '95 - The Woman With The Issue Of Blood	ST061	£3:00		
When The Trill Is All Gone	ST062	£3:00		
Whose Son Are You?	ST063	£3:00		
Why Bad Things Happen To Good People	ST064	£3:00		
Winning The Battle Before The Miracle	ST065	£3:00		
Wrong Signals	ST066	£3:00		
You Are As Good As Your Word	ST067	£3:00		
Your Time Has Come	ST068	£3:00		

Sub_Total _____
*Shipping _____
Total _____

* Shipping represents the cost of Postage and Packaging of the goods. Below are the various shipping rates.

	Country	Total Order Range	Shipping Cost
✍	**United Kingdom:**	for orders up to £15:00	10% of Total Order
		for orders up to £16:00 - £35:00	9% of Total Order
		for orders up to £36:00 -£50:00	8% of Total Order
		for orders up to £51:00 -£99:00	7% of Total Order
✍	**Outside United Kingdom:**		19% of Total Order
✍	**USA & Others:**		22% of Total Order

Supplimentary Order Form

Please fill out the order form and send to the address below

Name :

Address:

Post Code: **Country:**

Phone (H):   **(W):**

Item Code	Quantity	Amount
1.		
2.		
3.		
4.		
5.		
6.		
7.		
8.		
9.		
10.		
Postage & Packaging		
Total		

Mode of Payment:

❏ Cash   ❏ Cheque   ❏ Postal Order   ❏ Credit Card

Card Type: ❏ Access   ❏ Mastercard   ❏ Visa   ❏ Delta
                 ❏ Switch   (issue # ❏)

Card #: _ _ _ _   _ _ _ _   _ _ _ _   _ _ _ _   _ _ _

Expiry Date: _ _ / _ _

Mail to:- **KICC Bookstores Ltd, 1 Darnley Road, Hackney, London, E9 6QH ☎ 0181 525 0000**

PETITIONING GOD IN PRAYER

NAME (MR & MRS, MR, MRS, MISS):

Marquez Multon and Margaret Multon

ADDRESS:

TOWN:

COUNTY: POST CODE:

PHONE (H):

    (W):

*Let us join our faith with yours for your prayer needs, Fill out the
space below and send to the address given*

YOUR PETITION

1. Fruit of the wombs
2. House in N. California 3 bedroom
3. Financial Blessing, end to debt
4. Church home near to where I live
5. Permanent Job in Nursing CA
6. Midwifery certification in USA
7. Church home near to where I live
8. Speedy end to my settlement
9.
10.

MAIL TO:-

Kingsway International Christian Centre

1 Darnley Road, Off Mare Street, Hackney, London, E9 6QH.

If you want prayer immediately, call HOPELINE on **0181 525 0000**

PERSONAL DETAILS

NAME (MR & MRS, MR, MRS, MISS):

ADDRESS:

TOWN:

COUNTY: POST CODE:

PHONE   (H)
          (W)

FOR YOUR INFORMATION

❑ Please send me your free magazine WINNING WAYS,

❑ Please put me on your mailing list,

❑ Please send me a information on Kingsway International School of Ministry (KISOM).

MAIL TO:-

Kingsway International Christian Centre

1 Darnley Road, Off Mare Street, Hackney, London, E9 6QH.